focus on the family® marriage series

D0367715

the abundant *marriage*

Gospel Light

Gospel Light is a Christian publisher dedicated to serving the local church. We believe God's vision for Gospel Light is to provide church leaders with biblical, user-friendly materials that will help them evangelize, disciple and minister to children, youth and families.

It is our prayer that this Gospel Light resource will help you discover biblical truth for your own life and help you minister to others. May God richly bless you.

For a free catalog of resources from Gospel Light, please call your Christian supplier or contact us at 1-800-4-GOSPEL *or* www.gospellight.com

PUBLISHING STAFF
Bill Greig III, Publisher
Dr. Elmer L. Towns, Senior Consulting Publisher
Bayard Taylor, M.Div., Senior Editor, Biblical and Theological Issues
Rosanne Moreland, Cover Designer
Debi Thayer, Internal Designer
Tom Stephen and **Virginia Starkey,** Contributing Writers

ISBN 0-8307-3320-5
© 2004 Focus on the Family
All rights reserved.
Printed in the U.S.A.

This marriage study series is pure Focus on the Family—
reliable, biblically sound and dedicated to reestablishing family values
in today's society. This series will no doubt help a multitude of couples
strengthen their relationship, not only with each other,
but also with God, the *creator* of marriage itself.

Bruce Wilkinson

Author, The BreakThrough Series: *The Prayer of Jabez*,
Secrets of the Vine and *A Life God Rewards*

In this era of such need, Dr. Dobson's team has produced solid,
helpful materials about Christian marriage. Even if they have been
through marriage studies before, every couple—married or engaged—
will benefit from this foundational study of life together. Thanks to
Focus on the Family for helping set us straight in this top priority.

Charles W. Colson

Chairman, Prison Fellowship Ministries

In my 31 years as a pastor, I've officiated at hundreds of weddings.
Unfortunately, many of those unions failed. I only wish the *Focus on the
Family Marriage Series* had been available to me during those years.
What a marvelous tool you as pastors and Christian leaders have
at your disposal. I encourage you to use it to assist those you
serve in building successful, healthy marriages.

H. B. London, Jr.

Vice President, Ministry Outreach/Pastoral Ministries
Focus on the Family

Looking for a prescription for a better marriage?
You'll enjoy this timely and practical series!

Dr. Kevin Leman

Author, *Sheet Music: Uncovering the Secrets of
Sexual Intimacy in Marriage*

The *Focus on the Family Marriage Series* is successful because it shifts the focus from how to fix or strengthen a marriage to *who* can do it. Through this study you will learn that a blessed marriage will be the happy by-product of a closer relationship with the *creator* of marriage.

Lisa Whelchel

Author, *Creative Correction* and
The Facts of Life and Other Lessons My Father Taught Me

In a day and age where the covenant of marriage is so quickly tossed aside in the name of incompatibility and irreconcilable differences, a marriage Bible study that is both inspirational and practical is desperately needed. The *Focus on the Family Marriage Series* is what couples are seeking. I give my highest recommendation to this Bible study series that has the potential to dramatically impact and improve marriages today. Marriage is not so much about finding the right partner as it is about being the right partner. These studies give wonderful biblical teachings for helping those who want to learn the beautiful art of being and becoming all that God intends in their marriage.

Lysa TerKeurst

President, Proverbs 31 Ministries
Author, *Capture His Heart* and *Capture Her Heart*

table of contents

foreword

The most urgent mission field on Earth is not across the sea or even across the street—it's right where you live: in your home and family. Jesus' last instruction was to "make disciples of all nations" (Matthew 28:19). At the thought of this command, our eyes look across the world for our work field. That's not bad; it's just not *all*. God intended the home to be the first place of Christian discipleship and growth (see Deuteronomy 6:4-8). Our family members must be the *first* ones we reach out to in word and example with the gospel of the Lord Jesus Christ, and the fundamental way in which this occurs is through the marriage relationship.

Divorce, blended families, the breakdown of communication and the complexities of daily life are taking a devastating toll on the God-ordained institutions of marriage and family. We do not need to look hard or search far for evidence that even Christian marriages and families are also in a desperate state. In response to the need to build strong Christ-centered marriages and families, this series was developed.

Focus on the Family is well known and respected worldwide for its steadfast dedication to preserving the sanctity of marriage and family life. I can think of no better partnership than the one formed by Focus on the Family and Gospel Light to produce the *Focus on the Family Marriage Series*. This series is well written, biblically sound and right on target for guiding couples to explore the foundation God has laid for marriage and to see Him as the role model for the perfect spouse. Through these studies, seeds will be planted that will germinate in your heart and mind for many years to come.

In our practical, bottom-line culture, we often want to jump over the *why* and get straight to the *what*. We think that by *doing* the six steps or *learning* the five ways, we will reach the goal. But deep-rooted growth is slower and more purposeful and begins with a well-grounded understanding of God's divine design. Knowing why marriage exists is crucial to making the how-tos more effective. Marriage is a gift from God, a unique and distinct covenant relationship through which His glory and goodness can resonate, and it is only through knowing the architect and His plan that we will build our marriage on the surest foundation.

God created marriage; He has a specific purpose for it, and He is committed to filling with fresh life and renewed strength each union yielded to Him. God wants to gather the hearts of every couple together, unite them in love and walk them to the finish line—all in His great grace and goodness.

May God, in His grace, lead you into His truth, strengthening your lives and your marriage.

Gary T. Smalley
Founder and Chairman of the Board
Smalley Relationship Center

introduction

At the beginning of creation God "made them male and female." "For this reason a man will leave his father and mother and be united to his wife, and the two will become one flesh." So they are no longer two, but one.
Mark 10:6-8

The Abundant Marriage can be used in a variety of situations, including small-group Bible studies, Sunday School classes or counseling or mentoring situations. An individual couple can also use this book as an at-home marriage-building study.

Each of the four sessions contains four main components.

Session Overview

Tilling the Ground

This is an introduction to the topic being discussed—commentary and questions to direct your thoughts toward the main idea of the session.

Planting the Seed

This is the Bible study portion in which you will read Scripture and answer questions to help discover lasting truths from God's Word.

Watering the Hope

This is a time for discussion and prayer. Whether you are using the study at home as a couple, in a small group or in a classroom setting, talking about the lesson with your spouse is a great way to solidify the truth and plant it deeply in your hearts.

Harvesting the Fruit

As a point of action, this portion of the session offers suggestions on putting the truth of the Word into action in your marriage relationship.

Suggestions for Individual Couple Study

There are at least three options for using this study as a couple.

- It may be used as a devotional study that each spouse would study individually through the week; then on a specified day, come together and discuss what you have learned and how to apply it to your marriage.
- You might choose to study one session together in an evening and then work on the application activities during the rest of the week.
- Because of the short length of this study, it is a great resource for a weekend retreat. Take a trip away for the weekend, and study each session together, interspersed with your favorite leisure activities.

Suggestions for Group Study

There are many ways that this study can be used in a group situation. The most common way is in a small-group Bible study format. However, it can also be used in an adult Sunday School class. However you choose to use it, there are some general guidelines to follow for group study.

- Keep the group small—five to six couples is probably the maximum.
- Ask couples to commit to regular attendance for the four weeks of the study. Regular attendance is a key to building relationships and trust in a group.
- Encourage participants *not* to share anything of a personal or potentially embarrassing nature without first asking the spouse's permission.

- Whatever is discussed in the group meetings is to be held in strictest confidence among group members only.

There are additional leader helps in the back of this book and in *The Focus on the Family Marriage Ministry Guide*.

Suggestions for Mentoring or Counseling Relationships

This study also lends itself for use in relationships where one couple mentors or counsels another couple.

- A mentoring relationship, where a couple that has been married for several years is assigned to meet on a regular basis with a younger couple, could be arranged through a system set up by a church or ministry.
- A less formal way to start a mentoring relationship is for a younger couple to take the initiative and approach a couple that exemplifies a mature, godly marriage and ask them to meet with them on a regular basis. Or the reverse might be a mature couple that approaches a younger couple to begin a mentoring relationship.
- When asked to mentor, some might shy away and think that they could never do that, knowing that their own marriage is less than perfect. But just as we are to disciple new believers, we must learn to disciple married couples to strengthen marriages in this difficult world. The Lord has promised to be "with you always" (Matthew 28:20).
- Before you begin to mentor a couple, first complete the study yourselves. This will serve to strengthen your own marriage and prepare you for leading another couple.
- Be prepared to learn as much or more than the couple(s) you will mentor.

There are additional helps for mentoring relationships in *The Focus on the Family Marriage Ministry Guide*.

The *Focus on the Family Marriage Series* is based on Al Janssen's *The Marriage Masterpiece* (Wheaton, IL: Tyndale House Publishers, 2001), an insightful look at what marriage can—and should—be. In this study, we are pleased to lead you through the wonderful journey of discovering the joy in your marriage that God wants you to experience!

living *by* design

So God created man in his own image, in the image of God he created him;
male and female he created them. God blessed them and said to them,
"Be fruitful and increase in number; fill the earth and subdue it. Rule over
the fish of the sea and the birds of the air and over every living
creature that moves on the ground."
Genesis 1:27-28

During the bombing raids of World War II, thousands of children were orphaned and left to starve. The fortunate ones were rescued and placed in refugee camps where they were fed and cared for. But many of these children could not sleep at night. They feared waking up to find themselves once again homeless and without food. Nothing seemed to reassure them. Finally, someone gave each child a piece of bread to hold at bedtime. Holding their bread, these children finally slept in peace. All through the night the bread reminded them, *Today I ate and I will eat again tomorrow.*[1]

Many of us operate like those orphaned children, constantly worrying about having enough of what we need, or think we need. Individual fears about our limited resources prevent us from operating as a team with our spouse, and as stress and anxiety build, our marriage suffers. The not enoughs take their toll:

- Not enough time to get everything done
- Not enough money
- Not enough sleep or rest
- Not enough conversation to feel close to your spouse
- Not enough opportunities to have fun with your family
- Not enough . . .

Well, you get the idea!

Here's the good news: We have been given something even more reassuring than the bread that calmed the orphaned children after World War II. God has given each of us *more* than enough to provide for our every need. In return, we are to serve as stewards of what we have been given.

As you study God's Word, you and your spouse will receive the necessary tools for building a marriage that will not simply survive but will also thrive. Life will no longer be determined by the not enoughs—instead, it will be determined by God's amazing abundance.

tilling the ground

Our culture defines people as consumers; God's Word defines people as stewards. What's the difference?

- Consumers consume things; stewards care for things.
- Consumers seek more and better; stewards find satisfaction in what they have.
- Consumers seek peace through the acquisition of resources; stewards find peace from knowing resources will be provided.
- Consumers never have enough; stewards have more than enough.

Today's society beckons, entices and even demands that we view ourselves as consumers. Every day, billboards, television and radio commercials and magazine advertisements attempt to lure us into thinking that what we have is not good enough and that in order to be truly happy we need more—of everything. God's Word calls us to define ourselves as stewards.

1. Do you see yourself primarily as a consumer or a steward?

2. Check the box next to the statement in each section that best describes how you and your spouse feel about each issue.

   - Material possessions

     ❑ It is important that we have the best things available and to upgrade them regularly.
     ❑ We know most things are replaceable, but we keep what we can.
     ❑ We only replace those things we have to and prefer to take care of what we have.

- Necessities

  - ❑ We make sure we have what we need—if we don't take care of us, who will?
  - ❑ We know that God will take care of the big things, but we still worry over the details.
  - ❑ We trust that God will provide for all we need, and we trust His guidance to bring us where we need to be to receive His blessings.

- Contentment

  - ❑ Creature comforts are very important to us.
  - ❑ We would rather have quality than quantity.
  - ❑ Everything we have is a gift from God and what we have is sufficient for our needs.

3. In what areas, if any, do you feel anxiety because you don't feel you have enough?

As we study the story of creation and hear the words of Jesus, we'll uncover the secrets to living life as a good steward in an all-consuming world (pardon the pun).

 planting the seed

You must practice the basics if you want to succeed in any area of life, including marriage. Knowing the basics is essential to having an abundant marriage. Have you ever thought about what the basics are when it comes to marriage? God has, and He gave us His plan when He first created Adam and Eve.

The Garden of Eden was not created simply as a place for Adam and Eve to lie around and eat their favorite fruit. When God created the first couple, He did so for His purpose.

4. What does Genesis 1:26 tell us about God's purpose for Adam and Eve?

5. How does being created in God's image help you to fulfill your purpose?

Throughout the Old Testament, ruling over someone typically referred to a master's power over his or her servants.

6. Read Mark 10:42-45. Explain how Jesus' statement contradicted the traditional roles of master and servant up to that point.

Why do you think it is so important that we serve each other?

While Genesis 1—2:3 paints an overview of God creating the earth, Genesis 2 gives a more intimate and detailed account of the creation of man and woman.

As you read the account of the creation of our world, you will notice that it is continually stated that human beings were designed to take care of the world God created (see Genesis 1:26-28; 2:5-7,15,18).

Note: The Hebrew words used to describe how God defines our purpose on the earth include *abad* (see Genesis 2:5), *parah* and *rabah* (see Genesis 1:28). "Abad" can be translated "to work or serve."[2] Man was placed on the earth to act as a servant, taking care of the things God had created. "Parah" can be translated as "be fruitful,"[3] and "rabah" as "multiply, increase and become great."[4] God not only designed man to work the earth, but He also intends for us to enjoy His many provisions!

7. Read Genesis 1:28-29; 2:4-9 and then describe the ways in which God provides for you and your spouse.

8. What does James 1:17 say about the way God provides for us?

God's design for marriage is that you become "one flesh" with your spouse (Genesis 2:24). This includes becoming copartners in stewardship, taking care of everything you have been blessed with by God. Have you ever thought about how your marriage might change if you were to view the resources you have as a gift from God, given to you so that you might care for His creation? Think about it as you go through this study. Open your heart and your mind to the possibilities of how God has blessed you and how you can serve Him.

9. After reading Matthew 6:25-34, explain in your own words the point Jesus was making.

What did Jesus mean when He said, "Seek first his kingdom and his righteousness, and all these things will be given to you as well" (v. 33)?

watering the hope

Read the following story about Eric and Denise:

Eric and Denise each grew up in a home where money was scarce and a good work ethic was instilled by their parents—along with a fear that what little money they had would run out.

Both remembered hearing their parents argue about paying the bills, trying to figure out which bills to pay and which ones to hold off for just one more month. When Eric and Denise got married, they determined that they would not argue over money like their parents did. Both took well-paying jobs, and they worked together to stay on top of their finances. Not understanding why, Eric and Denise felt compelled to tell their friends and family how well they were doing financially. It seemed to everyone around them that their main topic of conversation was money in one form or another. Little did Eric and Denise know that their happiness was fleeting and that so much could change so quickly.

The first blow to their financial security occurred when Eric was laid off from his job. Eric received a three-month severance package and was sure he could find another good-paying job with time to spare. *In fact*, he thought, *I think I'll take a little vacation before I hit the pavement.* After a two-week vacation, Eric decided to go job hunting. Driving to an interview, Eric was rear-ended at a traffic light and suffered a life-threatening injury to his spine that required immediate surgery, months in the hospital and two years of rehabilitation.

The savings accounts Eric and Denise were so proud of quickly faded away, and they began to fear that they would lose their house. A friend heard about their hardship and approached his pastor to see if there was anything the church could do to help out. The pastor took the matter to the elders of the church, who unanimously voted to give Eric and Denise enough money to cover their mortgage payment for three months.

Eric and Denise, beside themselves with amazement over the gift they had been given, began to visit their friend's church. Soon they considered their friend's church as their own. Eric eventually found a job in a new field, and although the job did not pay as much as his previous one, Eric was satisfied because the job provided for what he and Denise needed.

Today, Eric and Denise are different people because they have felt God's hand providing for them. Although they are not as wealthy as they once were, they would not trade anything for the security they found in trusting God.[5]

10. What was the real cause of the fear with which both Eric and Denise were raised?

11. Have you ever experienced fear of not having enough of something? Was it something you needed or something you wanted so badly you *thought* you needed it?

Were your fears justified in the end, or were your needs met?

If five frogs are sitting on a lily pad and four plan to jump into the water, how many are left on the pad? One, right? Wrong.

The answer is that there are still five frogs on the lily pad. If they only *intend* to jump and never do it, nothing changes.

Are you ready to make the jump from being a consumer to become a steward?

Step One: Prepare to Jump (Be Thankful)

Thirteenth-century Dominican theologian Meister Johannes Eckhart is reported to have stated that if all we do is utter a word of thanksgiving, we have said enough. Begin this adventure into stewardship with daily prayers of thanks for God's provision.

Commit with your spouse to taking a five-day being-thankful challenge. Fill in the following chart for the next five days. Before you go to bed each night, share what you've written for that day with your spouse. You may be thankful for the same thing each day, but try each day to add at least two or three new things. Have fun and be creative!

Day One	Day Two	Day Three	Day Four	Day Five
I am thankful for	I am thankful for	I am thankful for	I am thankful for	I am thankful for

Step Two: Jump (Seek God First)

Brainstorm with your spouse some ways that you can seek God's kingdom first. As you consider all of the ideas, choose one discipline that you and your spouse will practice for the remainder of this study. Write your names in the space provided and then write down the discipline you have decided to follow.

We, _____ and _____,
plan to _____ for the remainder of this study in order to learn how to seek God's kingdom first in our lives.

Step Three: Hit the Water (Tend to Your Stress)

Number the following items from 1 to 7 (with 1 being the most stressful and 7 being the least stressful) to rate the amount of stress each creates in your marriage:

_____ Use of money
_____ Use of time
_____ Relationship with my spouse
_____ Relationships with friends
_____ Relationship with other family members
_____ Using individual gifts and talents
_____ Work responsibilities and pressures

Over the next three sessions, we are going to take a look at God's guidelines to address these potentially stressful issues. Commit to praying each day with your spouse for the top three issues that cause stress in your marriage. Then get ready, because your marriage will begin to thrive when you pursue the great adventure of stewardship and living in God's abundance!

Notes

1. Dennis Linn, Sheila Fabricant Linn, and Matthew Linn, *Sleeping with Bread: Holding What Gives You Life* (Mahwah, NY: Paulist Press, 1995), n.p.

2. *The New Strong's Exhaustive Concordance of the Bible* (Nashville, TN: Thomas Nelson Publishers, 1984), #5647.

3. Ibid., #6509.

4. Ibid., #7235.

5. This is a fictional account. Any resemblance to actual events or any people, living or dead, is purely coincidental.

If we only had *a little more . . .*

Do not store up for yourselves treasures on earth, where moth and rust destroy, and where thieves break in and steal. But store up for yourselves treasures in heaven, where moth and rust do not destroy, and where thieves do not break in and steal. For where your treasure is, there your heart will be also.

Matthew 6:19-21

Let's take a look at a typical day of a woman living in the African country of Sierra Leone. Talk about a full day's work!

4 A.M.	Wake up and start day by fishing in the local pond.
6 A.M.	Light the fire, heat water for washing, cook breakfast, wash dishes and sweep compound.
8 A.M.	Work in rice fields with two children, carrying one on her back.
11 A.M.	Collect berries, leaves and bark. Carry, along with water, back to compound.
NOON	Process and prepare food, cook lunch and wash dishes.
2 P.M.	Wash clothes, carry water to compound, clean and smoke fish.
3 P.M.	Work in the family garden.
5 P.M.	Fish again in the local pond.
6 P.M.	Process and prepare food; then cook dinner.
8 P.M.	Wash dishes and bathe children.
9 P.M.	Shell seeds and make fishnets while visiting with neighbors around the fire.

11 P.M.   Go to bed (on the ground).[1]

Imagine how much time this woman could save if she only had a washing machine, a stove, running water, a dishwasher, a local grocery store and a fast-food restaurant! Do you have any of these? Of course you do—if not all; at the very least you have running water, a stove and some place to shop for groceries. Think about your life: Does having these conveniences save you time, or are you just as busy as the woman in Sierra Leone? That's the great paradox of a consumer culture: We have all these things to make our lives easier, yet we're still incredibly busy.

What is true about time is also true about money. Have you ever thought about how much money you would have to earn to feel comfortable about your finances? Most people say that if only they could make 15 to 20 percent more money, they would be satisfied. The harsh truth is that you'd be hard pressed to find one person, whether that person makes $10,000 or $250,000 per year, who feels that he or she has enough.

The not enoughs and if onlys can take their toll on a marriage—but the good news is that they don't have to. God's Word gives us clear and helpful guidelines to help us understand how we can be good stewards of our time and our money.

 tilling the ground

1. Let's look at *your* typical day. Use the following two-hour incremental schedule to chart how you typically spend your day:

4 A.M.	_____
6 A.M.	_____
8 A.M.	_____
10 A.M.	_____
NOON	_____
2 P.M.	_____
4 P.M.	_____

6 P.M.	_____
8 P.M.	_____
10 P.M.	_____
MIDNIGHT	_____

Which one aspect of your daily schedule would you change if you could?

2. How much time do you spend with your spouse each day?

We are going to talk about the importance of the Sabbath in the next section of this week's study. Right now, let's consider how much time you spend in quiet time with God on a *daily* basis.

3. How much time do you spend in prayer and meditation each day?

You make appointments to see your doctor and dentist, an appointment to get your car serviced—you probably even make an appointment to get your hair cut. Have you ever thought about making an appointment each day to spend time with God?

4. How might your not enoughs and if onlys change if you were to make (and keep) an appointment with God every day?

5. Check the box that best describes how well you and your spouse communicate about money (e.g., how to spend it, how much to save).

    ❑ We don't agree on *any* money issues.
    ❑ More often than not, we argue when we discuss money.
    ❑ We are working on our communication regarding money and have made progress in this area since we first met.
    ❑ The money issue is not a problem for us because we have the same basic opinion about spending and saving it.

6. On what are you personally inclined to spend money?

On what are you and your spouse together inclined to spend money?

7. Do you and your spouse share equal responsibility for your finances? If not, who is primarily in charge and why?

Imagine that you've been hired to do a job specifically created to suit your unique gifts and talents. Not only is it a custom job designed just for you, but you have also been guaranteed a paycheck that will cover exactly what you need for the rest of your life. On your first day at work, your boss meets you at the door and says, "Welcome! Now you can go home and relax. We have a special policy for every employee's first day—it's also your first paid holiday. See you tomorrow!"

Sounds pretty good, doesn't it?

The Joy of Rest

Genesis 2:3 tells us that "God blessed the seventh day and made it holy, because on it he rested from all the work of creating that he had done." When God makes something holy, He sets it apart. The Bible is holy because the books that compose it have been set apart as God's Word. A sanctuary is holy because that building has been set apart for worship. What was it that made the seventh day holy, distinguishing it from all the other days? Rest!

8. What lesson might God have been trying to teach Adam and Eve by blessing their first full workday as a day of rest?

9. How might taking a day to rest and honor God set you apart from the mainstream of today's culture?

The Hebrew word for rest is *shabbat*, which not only means to rest or to cease, but also carries a sense of completion.[2] The word for the seventh day is *yom shabbat*.[3] The number seven in the Hebrew Scriptures is often associated with completion, fulfillment and perfection. Thus, God's work of creation was completed when God rested.

The people of Israel were called by God to be His people. The Old Testament tells the story of God showing His people how to follow Him and live the life that He created for them.

10. Write out Exodus 20:8-11 in your own words.

How might you live out this command within your marriage?

When we honor the Sabbath, we are reminded that our time is not ours to do with as we please. Each week, God calls us to rest from our busyness to remember that we are not in control of our lives—*He* is.

While honoring the Sabbath means resting one day a week, you can also take time during the week to gain perspective and consider the gifts God has given you. By stopping to rest regularly, we can remind ourselves that the world will continue to run without us (as much as we might like to think otherwise!).

Remember Jesus' words in Matthew 6:33: "But seek first his kingdom and his righteousness, and all these things will be given to you as well."

11. Is it difficult for you to take a complete day to rest and honor God? Why or why not?

The Tyranny of Success

Part of the struggle of giving our time over to God is that we are simply too busy trying to be successful, putting in long hours at work to make more money to pursue our materialistic ideals (i.e., the best looking house on the block, the most luxurious car, the latest gadgets and toys, the most exciting family vacation, and so on). We intentionally try to fill our personal treasure chests.

Jesus had a lot to say about treasure and what makes us happy. One day Jesus walked away from His very busy life and went up on a mountain. When His close friends found Him, He began to teach them ways to live a life that would bring them real joy.

12. Read Matthew 6:19-21 and think about the treasures you pursue as an individual. What do these treasures say about you?

   What treasures do you pursue with your spouse? What do these treasures say about you as a married couple?

Jesus said, "No one can serve two masters. Either he will hate the one and love the other, or he will be devoted to the one and despise the other. You cannot serve both God and Money" (Matthew 6:24). The term "money" does not just refer to currency and coins—even if you don't have money (or a lot of it), you *have* been given resources by God with which to serve Him and others.

13. Describe what a marriage devoted to serving money would look like.

Now describe how that same marriage would look if the couple were to serve God with their money.

A steward is someone who manages someone else's money. By analogy, God gives His people resources, making His people stewards of His resources!

14. What do the following passages tell you about how God desires His people to steward their money?

Psalm 37:21

Proverbs 22:9

Luke 12:13-21

Luke 12:41-48

1 Corinthians 4:2

2 Corinthians 9:6-11

1 Timothy 6:17-19

God has blessed you with a marriage in which you can experience joy and satisfaction. Not only has He given you and your spouse the task of caring for the time and resources you've been given, but He has also provided everything you need to perform that task.

Consider the true story of Tom and Ginny:

> "Things will be different once we're married," Tom said to Ginny as they walked down the beach on one of their rare evenings together.
>
> "Oh really?" Ginny replied with a bit of skepticism. "How so?"
>
> "Well, right now we're both working a lot to save money for our wedding and honeymoon. Naturally we're going to have more time to talk and hang out together once we're married and living in the same house!"
>
> "I hope you're right," his fiancée responded.
>
> A year later, the newlyweds rarely saw each other. The time pressures Tom had said would be lessened had in fact increased until the couple worked a combined 115 hours per week.
>
> Pregnant with their first child and frustrated over their situation, Tom's lonely wife entertained the idea of filing for divorce.[4]

15. What advice would you have given Tom and Ginny had you been walking with them that day on the beach? What could they have changed so that spending time together was a higher priority to them?

16. How can engaged or married couples honor God with their time and money?

As you think about what you've learned thus far in this study, it's important to consider how you can apply what you have learned to your own life. Remember: It is *action*—not the *intent* to act—that changes things.

17. Brainstorm with your spouse and use the following left-hand column to list two areas in which you and your spouse can improve in your use of your time, and two areas in which you can improve in your use of your money. Then in the right-hand column write the reasons you should make each change.

Now that you have identified some areas in which you and your spouse can work together to improve your use of time and money, it's time to work out some details for implementing a change in those areas!

18. Choose one item in each area you listed, and together with your spouse decide on four action steps you can take to make each change (see example).

Example

Honor the Sabbath

- Action Step One: Talk ahead of time with my spouse about how to do this.
- Action Step Two: Tell another couple about our intent and ask the couple to help keep us accountable.
- Action Step Three: Plan our Sabbath day ahead of time and stick to our plan.
- Action Step Four: Honor the Sabbath with rest, Bible study and worshiping God.

Use of Time

Action Step One: _____

Action Step Two: _____

Action Step Three: _____

Action Step Four: _____

Use of Money

Action Step One: _____

Action Step Two: _____

Action Step Three: _____

Action Step Four: _____

Now that you have a plan, set up a date this week at which time you and your spouse will come back together to talk about the commitments you made. We've said it before, and we're saying it again: It is not the intent that makes things happen—it's the action!

Notes

1. David Beckmann and Arthur Simon, *Grace at the Table* (Downers Grove, IL: InterVarsity Press, 1999), p. 97.

2. Howard I. Marshall, A. R. Millard, J. I. Packer, and D. J. Wiseman, gen. eds., *New Bible Dictionary, 3rd ed.* (Downers Grove, IL: InterVarsity Press, 1996), pp. 834-835.

3. Ibid.

4. We are happy to report that Tom and Ginny's marriage not only survived but also flourished as they learned to place time with God and each other at the top of their priority list. Their story is printed with permission.

one relationship *at a time*

Do nothing out of selfish ambition or vain conceit, but in humility consider others better than yourselves. Each of you should look not only to your own interests, but also to the interests of others. Your attitude should be the same as that of Christ Jesus.
Philippians 2:3-5

Have you ever felt used or taken for granted by others? Perhaps you worked too many hours for too little money only to be tossed aside because of corporate downsizing. Perhaps you had a one-sided friendship in which you made all the effort. Perhaps you burned out serving in ministry because no matter how hard you tried, people would only point out what needed improving. Perhaps you feel your spouse takes you for granted.

Within marriages, the Church and our culture, relationships break down when people treat others as commodities to be consumed. In a culture where the consumer is king, you may even be applauded for using someone else to meet your own personal needs and desires.

Stewards walk a different road. Rather than consuming relationships, stewards intentionally nurture relationships as gifts given into their care. In return, stewards experience life the way God intended. In this week's study, we're going to take a look at God's plan for the relationships in your life, including your marriage.

tilling the ground

Before we jump into this week's study, let's take some time to explore the difference between consuming relationships and stewarding relationships.

1. Briefly write about a relationship in which you experienced feeling like a commodity. How did being treated this way make you feel?

2. Briefly write about a relationship in which you felt cared for and protected. How was this feeling different from that of being a commodity?

3. Rate the following relationships in order of how important each is to living a fulfilled life (with 1 being most important and 7 being least important):

    _____ Relationship with parents
    _____ Relationship with church
    _____ Relationship with spouse
    _____ Relationship with God
    _____ Relationship with friends
    _____ Relationship with coworkers or boss
    _____ Relationship with strangers

Now think about your average day. Rate the same relationships based on how much effort you put into them (with 1 being most effort and 7 being least effort).

   _____ Relationship with parents
   _____ Relationship with church
   _____ Relationship with spouse
   _____ Relationship with God
   _____ Relationship with friends
   _____ Relationship with coworkers or boss
   _____ Relationship with strangers

One of the greatest paradoxes of human relationships is that we often hurt those who are closest to us, but then show kindness and compassion to others we barely know. We've all done it. Does the following scenario sound familiar?

> Steve was running late for a meeting but had to stop at the gas station. While waiting for his credit-card receipt to print, he spotted an older woman struggling to unscrew her gas cap. Steve offered to help and soon found himself encouraging the woman to get back into her car and let him pump the gas for her.
>
> Later that evening, while Steve was relaxing and watching the third quarter of the basketball game, his wife, Susan, called out to him, asking if he would help her by getting their young son out of the bath and dried off, so she could go into the kitchen and start dinner. Annoyed, Steve remarked that he had worked all day and was *just* getting to relax.
>
> Brusquely passing her in the hallway on his way to the bathroom, Steve never saw the hurt in Susan's eyes from his selfish remark.

The names and circumstances may be different, but no doubt you have experienced this scenario at some point in either the giving or receiving role. God's plan for your life is to show the love of Jesus not only to strangers but also to people whom you know—including your spouse. In your marriage, you and your spouse have been called to partner together to serve one another and others.

planting the seed

God's Overall Plan for Relationships

While sitting in a prison cell, a pastor heard that one of the churches he had planted was experiencing some difficulties. The church had its humble roots in an outdoor prayer gathering that had continued to grow, and church members had continually demonstrated Jesus' love by caring for the needs of others. But now, the pastor heard that division and conflict were occurring in the congregation. People were using others in order to get their way or to promote their cause. The pastor deeply cared for the people of this church— something had to be done.

The city? Philippi. The pastor? Paul. Thankfully, Paul did not mince words; and because of this, his letter to the Philippians contains instructions for living out God's plan as good stewards of our relationships.

4. List the phrases from Philippians 2:1-5 that speak about relationship with God and with others.

Almost every phrase in this passage tells us something about stewarding relationships. In Philippians 2, Paul continued to expand on the thought he had begun in Philippians 1:27: "Whatever happens, conduct yourselves in a manner worthy of the gospel of Christ."

Read Philippians 2:1-2. Notice that several phrases begin with the word "if," but the "if" is not used "the way we normally use it—as the condition upon which what follows depends."[1] Instead, Paul was outlining how we should act because we have already experienced these benefits in Christ.

5. Why would Paul begin his instructions on God-designed relationships by reminding the Philippians of the benefits they've experienced following Christ?

6. Describe how you have experienced or have seen others experience the following benefits as Paul listed them in Philippians 2:1:

Encouragement from being united with Christ

Comfort from His love

Fellowship with the Spirit

Tenderness and compassion

After describing the benefits of following Christ, Paul requested that the Philippians make his joy complete by "being like-minded, having the same love, being one in spirit and purpose" (v. 2). Paul didn't ask the Philippians to agree on every issue—but he was adamant that they have the same attitude when it came to caring for people.

7. Why would Paul's joy have been complete if the Philippians became united in their understanding of relationships?

How would you and your spouse become more united if you were to demonstrate the same attitude that Paul was encouraging the believers in Philippi to have?

God's Design for Being a Steward of Our Relationships

Philippians 2:3-5 provides us with a great outline for acting as good stewards in our relationships. Let's take a look at some simple-yet-profound principles.

"Do nothing out of selfish ambition or vain conceit" (v. 3).

Paul also used the term "selfish ambition" in Philippians 1:17 to describe the behavior of those who were preaching for the sake of causing him trouble. Selfish ambition, or vain conceit, "stands at the heart of human fallenness, where self-interest and self-aggrandizement at the expense of others primarily dictate values and behaviors."[2] Selfish ambition treats people like commodities, consuming others for themselves.

8. In which area(s) do you treat your spouse with selfish ambition? (Check all that apply.)

- ❑ Household chores
- ❑ Sexual intimacy
- ❑ Career pursuits
- ❑ Caring for children
- ❑ Alone time
- ❑ Other _____

- ❑ Spending money
- ❑ Paying bills
- ❑ Leisure time
- ❑ Control over the TV remote control

9. What is one way that you and your spouse can work together this week so that you don't treat each other with selfish ambition?

"But in humility consider others better than yourselves" (v. 3).

Humility is one of the greatest and most misunderstood Christian virtues. In the Greco-Roman world in which Paul wrote, humility was viewed as a handicap or a weakness. When Jesus showed an understanding of humility different from the common thinking of that time, He was definitely going against the grain, but He didn't care. Jesus had such confidence in who He was and why He was here on this earth that He did not have to humiliate others in order to make Himself feel superior.

10. Is it difficult for you to show humility toward your spouse? Why or why not?

11. "Submit to one another out of reverence for Christ" (Ephesians 5:21). How might focusing on your personal relationship with Jesus Christ help you to humble yourself before your spouse?

How might this change in focus help you to humble yourself before others?

"Each of you should look not only to your own interests, but also to the interests of others" (v. 4).

Have you ever given what you thought was the perfect gift only to have the recipient receive it with little or no enthusiasm? It's often easier to assume that others want the same things we do than taking the time to find out what they need or desire.

12. Describe a time when your spouse took a genuine interest in your needs or desires. How did this make you feel?

13. Is it possible to take a genuine interest in the needs of others without forsaking your own needs? Why or why not?

"Your attitude should be the same as that of Christ Jesus" (v. 5).

To paraphrase this verse, you should have the same mind-set that Christ had when it came to relationships. Read verses 6 through 8 to discover what type of attitude Christ Jesus had.

14. How would you describe Jesus' attitude toward other people?

15. What do the following Scripture passages tell you about the best way to approach relationships with other people?

Mark 10:42-45

Matthew 18:2-4

Is it possible to have the attitude of Christ in all your relationships? No— at least it's not humanly possible. But it *is* possible with God. He is the only One who can give you the strength and the desire you need to accomplish what He has called you to do. God has not only demonstrated how to be a good steward, but He has also provided the way for you to do it.

John 16:7-15 describes the importance of the Holy Spirit in your life. When you give your life over to Jesus Christ, the Holy Spirit literally comes alongside you as a counselor to help you live as God intended.

16. How can knowing that the Holy Spirit empowers you to live the way God intended influence your approach to being a good steward of your relationships?

Have you experienced God's forgiveness and love in a personal way? Have you decided to place your life in His hands? Becoming a good steward of relationships begins with that decision. The next step is to prioritize your relationships.

The Priority of Your Relationships

The following relationship priority triangle, based on Ephesians 5—6, is a simple outline for prioritizing your relationships:

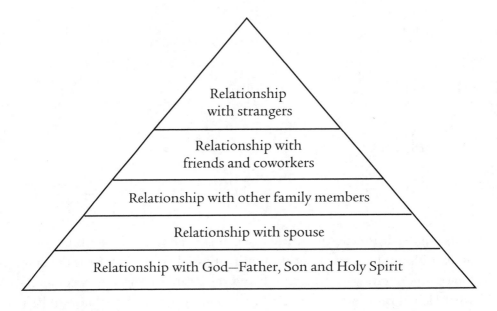

You establish a strong foundation for all other relationships by making a personal relationship with God your first priority. Every other relationship is built on that relationship. In his book *My Utmost for His Highest*, Oswald Chambers wrote: "Your priorities must be God first, God second, and God third, until your life is continually face-to-face with God and no one else is taken into account whatsoever."[3]

After Himself, God has called you to be faithful to your spouse. You move from the One who knows you the best, to the person with whom you have become one through marriage. Think about it: You are one with no one else on this earth other than your spouse! If you do not care for your marriage relationship, other relationships will be built on shaky ground.

After your spouse, your next priority is your relationship with other family members, and then relationships with people outside your family. God calls you to care for those who have been given directly into your care and then to move out to others.

17. Summarize what each of the following Scripture passages has to say about prioritizing your relationships:

Genesis 2:23-24

1 Timothy 3:4-5

1 Timothy 5:8

watering the hope

Consider Dave and Julie's story:

> After 30 years of marriage, Dave and Julie decided on a trial separation. Upon hearing the news about their breakup, neither their children nor their close friends were surprised. Most had seen it coming for a long time.
>
> Dave was a dedicated social worker and had invested many hours into the lives of his clients. Those he helped were continually commenting to Dave's supervisor that Dave was always available to address their concerns and problems. A certified public accountant, Julie worked part-time as an accounting secretary so that she could be at home with their three children as much as possible.
>
> As the years went by, Dave and Julie began to drift apart. It wasn't unusual for their children to fall asleep listening to the couple argue about either money or the fact that Dave gave so much of himself to strangers that he didn't have anything left to give to his family. Although they continued to attend church as a family, neither Dave nor Julie could remember the last time they had prayed together at home.
>
> When their youngest child headed off to college, the couple realized just how far they had distanced themselves from each other, and neither one held much hope that they could fix their broken marriage. After all, they reasoned, there was too much water under the bridge, and with the kids grown now, what was the point in staying together?[4]

18. What would Dave's relationship priority triangle look like?

Julie's?

How do the priorities shared by this couple compare with the priorities highlighted in Ephesians 5—6?

19. What should Dave and Julie do about their marriage? What advice would you give the couple?

20. Be honest with yourself and draw your relationship priority triangle. Where are your priorities at this point in your life?

21. Use the following scale to rate how much your relationship with God has changed thus far in this Bible study:

<u>1</u>   2   3   4   <u>5</u>

No change   Some change   Big change

22. List two practical ways in both attitude and action that you need to change in order to better care for your relationship with your spouse. (For example, you might list "notice and appreciate the little things my spouse does for me" as an attitude change and "spend at least 15 uninterrupted minutes with my spouse after dinner every night, sharing about our day" as an action change.)

Attitude

Action

23. Think about other relationships that you and your spouse have been called to care for (this could be family members, friends and coworkers—even people in other countries). What two ways can you serve these people in the next month?

When your relationships with others are built upon a firm foundation of a personal relationship with God, you will begin to treat others as precious gifts and not expendable commodities. In doing so, you will realize the full potential of every relationship in which God has placed you—and you will see His hand working in every aspect of your life (including your marriage).

Notes
1. Maxie D. Dunnam, *The Communicator's Commentary: Galatians, Ephesians, Philippians, Colossians, Philemon* (Waco, TX: The Word Books, 1982), p. 276.
2. Gordon D. Fee, *Paul's Letter to the Philippians: The New International Commentary of the New Testament* (Grand Rapids, MI: William B. Eerdmans Publishing, 1995), p. 186.
3. Oswald Chambers, *My Utmost for His Highest* (Grand Rapids, MI: Discovery House, 1992), p. 13.
4. This is a fictional account. Any resemblance to actual events or people, living or dead, is purely coincidental.

Gifting *it away*

Do not conform any longer to the pattern of this world, but be transformed by the renewing of your mind. Then you will be able to test and approve what God's will is—his good, pleasing and perfect will.
Romans 12:2

Do you have a most memorable Christmas gift? Most likely you do. One day Tom found a long-lost gift quite by accident.

> One July morning I was exploring some boxes in the attic in order to get ready for a garage sale. Most of the boxes were filled with "treasures" that I knew someone would love to add to their own collection.
>
> As I opened the last box, red wrapping paper caught my eye. I soon discovered a beautifully wrapped gift. I looked at the card and read "To Tommy from Mom, Merry Christmas." My mother had given me a gift with great love, and for some reason it had wound up unopened in the attic.[1]

Imagine uncovering a gift chosen especially for you that was simply waiting to be opened! Tom experienced this with a gift from his mom. God has given you gifts—individual and shared—and resources to be used for His kingdom. In many marriages those gifts remain unopened, undiscovered or unused. Part of God's command to "be fruitful and . . . multiply" (Genesis 9:7) is to use the gifts that God has given you to help multiply and bear fruit in His kingdom. As you discover and use your gifts together with your spouse, you will experience the joy of an abundant marriage that follows God's command to be wise stewards.

1. Describe your spouse's gifts and talents that first attracted you to him or her.

2. Describe married couples you know who use their gifts and resources as a team to serve others.

3. Complete the following sentences to define the different ways a consumer and a steward approach the use of gifts and resources:

   A consumer uses gifts and resources to _____.

   A steward uses gifts and resources to _____.

planting the seed

Howard Hughes was one of the most talented and resourceful men in America during the mid-twentieth century. He was also one of the most eccentric; he was never satisfied with his wealth or his accomplishments. Hughes had the world at his feet, yet he died virtually alone because most of his life was spent feeding his need to consume.

While very few of us will ever have the resources that Howard Hughes possessed, we've all been given gifts and resources. If the life of Howard Hughes serves as an extreme example of what happens when you spend your life as a consumer, how would a wise steward approach the use of gifts and resources? Let's take a look at what Jesus had to say about it.

4. Read Matthew 24:45-51. How did the servant in this story act as a consumer of the gifts and resources put under his charge?

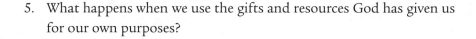

5. What happens when we use the gifts and resources God has given us for our own purposes?

6. What are some differences between the wise and unwise virgins in Matthew 25:1-13?

    What are some similarities?

    What does this parable make you think about regarding being ready to use your gifts and resources for God's purposes?

Now let's take a close look at Matthew 25:14-30. First, each servant was entrusted with property, each in an amount according to his ability. At the time Jesus told this story, it would take a day laborer 20 years to earn the equivalent of one talent, so even the servant who received the least amount from his master was given much to care for.

7. Did the master expect more from the servants to whom more had been given? Why or why not?

8. What are the fears the third servant might have experienced when considering how to use the resources he had been given?

Fear often prevents people from using their gifts and resources. We fear not having enough or not making right choices, and we worry about whether or not God will provide for us in the future.

9. Are you willing to use the gifts and resources that God has entrusted to you, or are you fearful that He won't provide for your needs again?

God has promised that if we obey His command to use our resources wisely, He will continue to provide for us abundantly.

10. In relation to the parable of the three servants, what did Jesus mean when He said, "For everyone who has will be given more, and he will have an abundance. Whoever does not have, even what he has will be taken from him" (v. 29)?

It is clear that Jesus is calling you to be a wise steward of the gifts and resources you've been given. So then how do you and your spouse become wise stewards? Romans 12:1-2 gives us the answer: Our entire life, including everything we have is to be used as a sacrifice to God. We are to offer ourselves and our resources to honor Him.

For most of us, offering God all that we have does not come naturally.

11. Describe how a person might use his or her gifts and resources to conform to the pattern of this world.

The word for "transformed" in Greek, *metamorfoo*, is the same word from which we derive the English word "metamorphosis."[2] A metamorphosis happens when one changes in appearance, character, condition or function. In the insect world, a metamorphosis takes place when a caterpillar becomes a butterfly. A metamorphosis can also occur in our lives.

12. In what way can adopting each of the following habits transform the way you use your gifts and resources to honor God?

Prayer

Scripture reading

Being a part of a community of faith

13. Read Romans 12:3. How can thinking too highly of yourself cause you to be an unwise steward?

How can not valuing your gifts and resources cause you to be an unwise steward?

While Paul's primary message in Romans 12:4-8 is how members of the Body of Christ offer unique gifts so that the Body functions well, the image of the body also relates to how we function in marriage.

14. According to Paul in Romans 12:4-8, how does being one body yet having different functions relate to how married couples should use their gifts and resources?

15. How does 1 Corinthians 12:14-26 illustrate the importance of different people with different gifts in the Body of Christ?

16. According to 1 Peter 4:8-11, how should a steward use his or her gifts?

Before we begin to unwrap some of the gifts God has given you and your spouse, read the following case study about two couples who attend the same weekly Bible study:

Steve and Margie have a reputation for giving. When their children outgrow clothes (and sometimes even *before* they do), they find a family who needs clothing. Although they have only one vehicle, Steve and Margie frequently allow the church to borrow their van for youth trips, and while they live on a very modest income, the couple loves to invite friends over for delicious meals. When friends offer to treat the couple to a restaurant dinner, they happily accept.

Someone recently asked the couple, "How is it so easy for you to give and receive?" Margie replied, "God takes care of us, and we have faith that things will work themselves out."

Steve and Margie's friends Karen and Michael are doctors, each in private practice. Each year, they have an out-with-the-old sale-a-thon. They use all the money from this garage sale as extra spending money for their annual summer vacation.

Karen and Michael have often wondered why their friends Margie and Steve are so willing to loan their van to the youth group. Karen and Michael can't imagine allowing a bunch of teenagers to mess up one of their vehicles! They reason that being good stewards of their automobiles means keeping them pristine so that they keep their maximum value. Karen and Michael enjoy spending time with their friends and often eat out. Extremely responsible with their money, the couple is always the first to be sure they pay their part of the bill at a restaurant.[3]

17. How do these two couples compare with the servants in the parable of the talents?

18. What spiritual gifts do you see evident in each couple?

19. Both couples in this case study believe they are being good stewards. What advice would you give each couple?

20. What characteristics of each couple do you see in your marriage?

harvesting the fruit

Considering Your Resources

Do you remember coming home from school as a teenager completely famished and heading straight for the kitchen cupboards and refrigerator to find something to eat? Most likely you also remember complaining at some point, "How come there is never anything to eat in this house?!" only to have your mom or dad list several things that could be eaten. A more accurate statement of exasperation would have been, "There is nothing in the kitchen that I want to eat."

This same scenario is sometimes played out in our adult lives too, when we fail to recognize the gifts and resources that we live with every day because we are looking for something different.

21. Place a check mark next to each resource you currently have at your disposal.

❏ Ability to listen   ❏ Musical instrument
❏ Ability to read and write   ❏ Place to live
❏ Clothes you don't wear   ❏ Savings and/or
❏ Computer   checking account(s)
❏ Education   ❏ Telephone
❏ Movie and/or music collection   ❏ Tools
❏ Transportation   ❏ Other: _____

Choose any three of the resources you checked and write down at least three ways each could be used to serve others (e.g., members of your family, coworkers, your community).

Resource One: _____

Resource Two: _____

Resource Three: _____

Exploring Your Gifts

According to Barna Research Group, 71 percent of people say they have heard of spiritual gifts. Of those people

- 12 percent claim they do not have a spiritual gift;
- 31 percent can name a spiritual gift they believe they possess. However, when asked to identify their spiritual gifts this group listed characteristics or qualities *not* identified as spiritual gifts in the Bible. The most common traits mentioned were love, kindness, relationships, singing and listening.[4]

If we are going to be good stewards of the spiritual gifts that we've been given, we need to have a clear understanding of those gifts.[5]

22. The following are some of the spiritual gifts that God has laid out in Scripture. Check the box next to the gifts that you think God may have given you and your spouse.

> ❑ Administration (see 1 Corinthians 12:28)
> ❑ Apostle (see 1 Corinthians 12:28)
> ❑ Discernment (see 1 Corinthians 12:10)
> ❑ Evangelism (see Ephesians 4:11)
> ❑ Exhortation (see Romans 12:8)
> ❑ Faith (see 1 Corinthians 13:2)
> ❑ Giving (see Romans 12:8)
> ❑ Healing (see 1 Corinthians 12:28)

- ❑ Helps (see 1 Corinthians 12:28)
- ❑ Hospitality (see 1 Peter 4:9-10)
- ❑ Interpretation (see 1 Corinthians 12:10)
- ❑ Knowledge (see 1 Corinthians 12:8)
- ❑ Leadership (see Romans 12:8)
- ❑ Mercy (see Romans 12:8)
- ❑ Missionary (see Acts 22:21; 1 Corinthians 9:19-23)
- ❑ Pastor (see Ephesians 4:11)
- ❑ Prophecy (see 1 Corinthians 12:28)
- ❑ Service (see 1 Peter 4:10)
- ❑ Teaching (see 1 Corinthians 12:28)
- ❑ Tongues (see 1 Corinthians 12:28)
- ❑ Voluntary poverty (see Acts 2:44–45, 4:34–47; James 2:5)

23. In what ways have you exercised the gifts that you checked over the past year?

In what ways have you neglected using them?

24. List several ways you can encourage your spouse to be a good steward of his or her gifts.

List several ways you might discourage your spouse from being a good steward (and then strive to avoid them!).

25. In what ways can you use the gifts you possess to complement your spouse?

26. Thinking about what you have learned about yourself and your marriage during this study, how would you like your marriage to be different one year from now regarding stewardship?

    What steps can you personally take to reach this goal? What steps can you take with your spouse?

Notes

1. This is a true story and is printed with permission.

2. "The NAS New Testament Greek Lexicon," *Crosswalk.com*.http://bible.crosswalk.com/Lexicons/ Greek/grk.cgi?number=3339&version=nas (accessed August 12, 2003).

3. This is a fictional account. Any resemblance actual events or people, living or dead, is purely coincidental.

4. George Barna, *Spiritual Gifts*, 2001. http://www.barna.org/cgi-bin/PageCategory.asp?CategoryID=35 (accessed July 22, 2003).

5. For a questionnaire designed to help you discover your spiritual gifts, refer to C. Peter Wagner, *Discover Your Spiritual Gifts* (Ventura, CA: Gospel Light, 2002).

leader's
discussion guide

General Guidelines

1. If at all possible, the group should be led by a married couple. This does not mean that both spouses need to be leading the discussions—perhaps one spouse is better at facilitating discussions while the other is better at relationship building or organization—but the leader couple should share responsibilities wherever possible.

2. At the first meeting, be sure to lay down the ground rules for discussions, stressing that following these rules will help everyone feel comfortable during discussion times.
   a. No one should share anything of a personal or potentially embarrassing nature without first asking his or her spouse's permission.
   b. Whatever is discussed in the group meetings is to be held in strictest confidence among group members only.
   c. Allow everyone in the group to participate. However, as a leader, don't force anyone to answer a question if he or she is reluctant. Be sensitive to the different personalities and communication styles among your group members.

3. Fellowship time is very important in building small-group relationships. Providing beverages and/or light refreshments either before or after each session will encourage a time of informal fellowship.

4. Most people live very busy lives; respect the time of your group members by beginning and ending meetings on time.

The Focus on the Family Marriage Ministry Guide has even more information on starting and leading a small group. You will find this an invaluable resource as you lead others through this Bible study.

How to Use the Material

1. Each session has more than enough material to cover in a 45-minute teaching period. You will probably not have time to discuss every single question in each session, so prepare for each meeting by selecting questions you feel are most important to address for your group; discuss other questions as time permits. Be sure to save the last 10 minutes of your meeting time for each couple to interact individually and to pray together before adjourning.

    Optional Eight-Session Plan—You can easily divide each session into two parts if you'd like to cover all of the material presented in each session. Each section of the session has enough questions to divide in half, and the Bible study sections (Planting the Seed) are divided into two or three sections that can be taught in separate sessions. (You'll find more on how to do this in *The Focus on the Family Marriage Ministry Guide*.)

2. Each spouse should have his or her own copy of the book in order to personally answer the questions. The general plan of this study is that the couples complete the questions at home during the week and then bring their books to the meeting to share what they have learned during the week.

    However, the reality of leading small groups in this day and age is that some members will find it difficult to do the homework. If you find that to be the case with your group, consider adjusting the lessons and having members complete the study during your meeting time as you guide them through the lesson. If you use this method, be sure to encourage members to share their individual answers with their spouses during the week (perhaps on a date night).

Session One | Living By Design

Before The Meeting

1. If couples do not already know each other and/or you do not already know everybody's name, gather material for making name tags.
2. Gather extra paper, pens or pencils, 3x5-inch index cards and Bibles, along with a white board, chalkboard or large piece of newsprint.
3. Make photocopies of the Prayer Request Form (see *The Focus on the Family Marriage Ministry Guide*, "Reproducible Forms" section) or provide 3x5-inch cards for recording requests. You may also want to have a notebook ready to record prayer requests and pray for each group member during the week.
4. Complete the study on your own during the week. Read through your own answers from the session and mark the ones that you specifically want the group to discuss. As you prepare your answers, pray that God would direct your discussion.
5. Prepare slips of paper with references for the verses that you will want someone to read aloud during the session. Distribute these slips as group members arrive, but be sensitive to those who are uncomfortable reading aloud or who might not be familiar with the Bible.

Ice Breakers

1. Distribute Prayer Request Forms (or index cards) to members as they enter the meeting room. Encourage them to complete their prayer requests before the session begins. (If they don't have a specific prayer request, they can just write their name on the paper so that another member can pray for them by name during the upcoming week.)
2. If this is the first meeting for this couples group, have everyone introduce themselves and give a brief summary of how they met their spouse, how long they've been married and one interesting fact about their spouse. (Be sure to remind couples not to reveal anything about their spouse that the spouse would be uncomfortable sharing about him- or herself.)
3. **Option 1:** Invite each couple to share about an exciting trip or activity they enjoyed together.

4. **Option 2:** Have each member share one characteristic, or quality, his or her spouse has that he or she respects.

5. Read the introduction together as a group.

Discussion

1. **Tilling the Ground**—Ask a volunteer to read the differences between consumers and stewards; then ask volunteers to share one of their answers from question 2. Be sure to share your answers—this will model an openness and vulnerability that will be necessary for couples to get the most out of this study. If no one else is willing to share, don't push it. Couples will grow more comfortable with sharing as time goes on.

2. **Planting the Seed**—Separate into small groups of two or three couples each and have members discuss the importance of serving one another and how that relates to stewardship of God's gifts, or taking care of the things God has given us.

3. **Watering the Hope**—Ask volunteers to share their answers to question 10 and have groups discuss the different ways in which fear can keep us from good stewardship over what God has given us.

   Ask volunteers to share their answers to question 11 and write responses on a white board, chalkboard or a sheet of newsprint. Point out that sometimes we can want something so much that we convince ourselves that we need it. Discuss how this mind-set can affect our trust that God will provide for our every need.

4. **Harvesting the Fruit**—Emphasize the importance of taking action steps each week through this study. Remind members that the study is simply laying the foundation for living out God's guidelines for stewardship. Discuss the importance of prayer and thanksgiving in our everyday life, and how each of the steps outlined in this section will help couples to become better stewards.

   The first step is designed to give each couple a practical way to begin daily thanksgiving. Ask members to commit to the five-day being-thankful challenge, and to end each day this week by sharing with their spouse what they have written for that day.

   The second step is designed to help couples seek God's kingdom first in their lives and in their marriage. They can choose to practice a discipline together or each spouse can choose one to practice on his or her own.

The third step is designed to help couples recognize areas in their life that are more stressful than others. In this way, they can prioritize and band together as a couple to tackle those things that are stressful.

5. **Close in Prayer**—An important part of any small-group relationship is time spent in prayer for one another. This may be done in a number of ways:

   a. Have members write out specific prayer requests on the Prayer Request Forms (or index cards). These may be shared with the whole group or traded with another couple as prayer partners for the week. If requests are shared with the whole group, pray as a group before adjourning the meeting; if requests are traded, allow time for the prayer-partner couples to pray together.

   b. Gather the whole group together and lead couples in guided prayer, asking that God will continue to give them guidance as they share the exciting plan God has for their lives.

   c. Have spouses pray together.

After The Meeting

1. **Evaluate**—Leaders should spend time evaluating the meeting's effectiveness (see *The Focus on the Family Marriage Ministry Guide* "Reproducible Forms" section for an evaluation form).

2. **Encourage**—During the week try to contact each couple (through phone calls, notes of encouragement, or e-mail or instant messaging) and welcome them to the group. Make yourself available for answering questions or concerns they may have, and use the opportunity to generally get to know them. This contact might best be done by the husband-leader contacting the men and the wife-leader contacting the women.

3. **Equip**—Complete session two of this study, even if you have previously gone through the study with your spouse.

4. **Pray**—Prayerfully prepare for the next meeting, praying for each couple and for your own preparation.

Session Two | If We Only Had a Little More . . .

Before The Meeting

1. Pray with your spouse and discuss how God has been working in your marriage over the past week.

2. Gather materials for making name tags in addition to extra paper, pens or pencils, 3x5-inch index cards and Bibles.

3. Make photocopies of the Prayer Request Form or provide index cards for recording requests. Bring your prayer journal or notebook and review prayer requests for the week. As people arrive, you can do an informal check-in or you can ask if anyone wants to share how God answered prayers during the past week.

4. Read through your own answers from the session and mark the ones that you specifically want the group to discuss. As you prepare, pray that God would direct the group discussion and give you insight into your own use of money and time.

5. Prepare slips of paper with the references for the verses that you will want someone to read aloud during the session. Again, be sensitive to those who prefer not to read aloud.

Note: Some people are very uncomfortable talking about money. You may want to acknowledge this up front, and then encourage others to be open by talking about your own hesitations to share, but that you are willing to risk it because you want to grow in this area.

Ice Breakers

1. Distribute Prayer Request Forms (or index cards) to members as they enter the meeting room. Encourage them to complete their prayer requests before the session begins.

2. **Option 1:** Give each member a blank sheet of paper and a pen or pencil. Have everyone write their answers to the following questions:
   - If you could add an extra four hours to your day, what would you do with the extra time?
   - If your employer offered to increase your salary to whatever

you asked for, what would the amount be and what would you do with the extra money?

3. **Option 2:** Have each couple share something they discovered during the five-day being-thankful challenge.

4. **Option 3:** Have members describe their typical day, including one thing they like and one thing they do not like about their routine.

5. Begin in prayer.

Discussion

1. **Tilling the Ground**—Have a volunteer read the daily schedule of the woman in Sierra Leone. Break into small groups and have members share their answers to the last part of question 1 and questions 4 and 7. As a whole group, discuss how difficult it can be to admit that we are not always the best stewards of our time or our money.

2. **Planting the Seed**—The challenge of this particular Bible study is that the issues of how to honor God with our time and our money could each be a six-week study on its own. Discuss questions 8 and 9. Point out that although we are commanded to take the Sabbath off, it is not so that we can become encumbered by yet another thing to do; it is so we can stop and rest, relaxing and reflecting on how God has provided for us.

   Ask volunteers to share what they learned from the Scripture references in question 14 to get members thinking about how God expects us to use our money. (You will be addressing this more in-depth in the next section.)

3. **Watering the Hope**—Break into small groups and have members discuss the advice they would have given the couple that day on the beach. Encourage them to come up with strategies that Tom and Ginny could have used to avoid the stress they brought on themselves before and after their wedding.

4. **Harvesting the Fruit**—Have members discuss their action plan (question 18).

5. **Close in Prayer**—Have couples pair up with another couple and share their prayer requests. Allow time for the prayer-partner couples to pray together and then close the meeting by praying for the couples.

After The Meeting

1. **Evaluate**—Spend time evaluating the meeting's effectiveness.
2. **Encourage**—During the week, try to contact each couple and encourage them to contact their prayer partners.
3. **Equip**—Complete session three of this study.
4. **Pray**—Prayerfully prepare for the next meeting, praying for each couple and your own preparation.

Session Three | One Relationship at a Time

Before the Meeting

1. Gather extra paper, pens or pencils, 3x5-inch index cards and Bibles.
2. Make photocopies of the Prayer Request Form or provide index cards for recording requests. Bring your prayer journal or notebook and review prayer requests for the week. As people arrive, you can do an informal check-in or you can ask if anyone wants to share how God answered prayers during the past week.
3. Read through your own answers from the session and mark the ones that you specifically want the group to discuss. Pray with your spouse, asking God which members of the group He may be calling you to care for specifically. As you prepare, pray that God would give you direction through the discussion.
4. Prepare slips of paper with references for the verses that you will want someone to read aloud during the session.

Ice Breakers

1. Distribute Prayer Request Forms (or index cards) to members as they enter the meeting room. Encourage them to complete their prayer requests before the session begins.
2. **Option 1:** Ask members to share two qualities they appreciate about their spouse.
3. **Option 2:** Ask volunteers to share about a relationship in which they felt responsible to care for someone.

Discussion

1. **Tilling the Ground**—Ask volunteers to share their answers to either question 1 or 2. Discuss question 3 and the importance of each relationship God has brought into our life.
2. **Planting the Seed**—Have members form small groups of two to three

couples each and discuss questions 5 and 6. Bring the group back together and discuss question 16 and the importance of allowing the Holy Spirit to guide us in our relationships.

As you work through this section, pray that God would reveal those in your group who have not yet made a decision to follow Christ. This study is designed to bring people into a relationship with Him, since the primary relationship we need to become good stewards is a relationship with God.

3. **Watering the Hope**—Discuss questions 18 and 19; then ask members to take a moment to discuss with their spouse whether or not their spouse is comfortable sharing his or her relationship priority triangle from question 20. Invite anyone who is comfortable sharing (and whose spouse does not object) to share the information from his or her triangle.

4. **Harvesting the Fruit**—Ask volunteers to share their answers to questions 21 and 22.

5. **Close in Prayer**—Have each couple pair with another couple and share their prayer requests. Allow time for couples to pray with their prayer partners; then close the meeting by praying for each couple individually.

After the Meeting

1. **Evaluate.**
2. **Encourage**—During the week, call each couple and ask if they have called their prayer partners this week. Encourage them as they continue to complete the study.
3. **Equip**—Complete the last session of this study.
4. **Pray**—Prayerfully prepare for the next meeting, praying for each couple and for your own preparation.

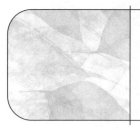

Reminder: God has called you and your spouse to be good stewards of the couples in your Bible study group. You will be modeling good stewardship as you interact with them. May God bless you as you care specifically for each member with the love of Christ!

Session Four | Gifting It Away

Before the Meeting

1. Gather extra paper, pens or pencils, 3x5-inch index cards and Bibles.
2. Make photocopies of the Prayer Request Form or provide index cards for recording requests.
3. Make photocopies of the Study Review Form (see *The Focus on the Family Marriage Ministry Guide*, "Reproducible Forms" section).
4. Read through your own answers from the session and mark the ones that you specifically want the group to discuss, particularly in the Planting the Seed section.
5. Prepare slips of paper with references for the verses that you will want someone to read aloud during the session.
6. Be sure that you have a good understanding of the descriptions of the different spiritual gifts listed in Harvesting the Fruit.

Ice Breakers

1. Distribute Prayer Request Forms (or index cards) to members as they enter the meeting room. Encourage them to complete their prayer requests before the session begins.
2. **Option 1:** Ask members each to answer one of the following questions:
   - What was the most surprising gift you have ever received?
   - What was the best gift you have ever received?
3. **Option 2:** Ask volunteers to share how this study has impacted their marriage and their understanding of God's abundant provision.
4. **Option 3:** Ask each member to answer question 1 in Tilling the Ground.
5. Begin the meeting in prayer, thanking God for all He has taught the group during this study and asking for guidance and grace during this last session.

Discussion

1. **Tilling the Ground**—Have each couple partner with one or two other couples to form small groups and discuss their answers to questions 2 and 3. Allow a few minutes for discussion; then ask a volunteer in each group to share some of the answers from question 3.
2. **Planting the Seed**—You may want to read all three parables in this section at once and then go back and read them individually to help group members see the big picture before you work through the details. Discuss the questions you chose to review.
3. **Watering the Hope**—Discuss ways in which each couple in the case study demonstrates good stewardship and ways in which each couple needs to improve. This is a great time to point out that advice can be given as encouragement and not admonishment.
4. **Harvesting the Fruit**—Encourage each group member to add one other item to the list in question 21. Have small groups discuss questions 24 and 26.
5. **Close in Prayer**—Use this time to bring some closure to the group. Pray together with the whole group and have couples pray specifically that the other couples grow deeper in their relationship with Jesus Christ. After prayer, take time to talk about what group members will do to continue to grow in their relationships with one another.

After the Meeting

1. **Evaluate**—Distribute the Study Review Forms for members to take home with them. Share about the importance of feedback, and ask members to take the time this week to write their review of the group meetings and then return it to you.
2. **Encourage**—Call each couple during the next week and invite them to join you for the next study in the *Focus on the Family Marriage Series*.
3. **Equip**—Begin preparing and brainstorming new activities for the next Bible study.
4. **Pray**—Praise the Lord for the work He has done in the lives of the couples in the study. Continue to pray for these couples as they apply the lessons learned in the last few weeks.

Welcome to the Family!

As you participate in the *Focus on the Family Marriage Series*, it is our prayerful hope that God will deepen your understanding of His plan for marriage and that He will strengthen your marriage relationship.

This series is just one of the many helpful, insightful, and encouraging resources produced by Focus on the Family. In fact, that's what Focus on the Family is all about—providing inspiration, information, and biblically based advice to people in all stages of life.

It began in 1977 with the vision of one man, Dr. James Dobson, a licensed psychologist and author of 18 best-selling books on marriage, parenting, and family. Alarmed by the societal, political, and economic pressures that were threatening the existence of the American family, Dr. Dobson founded Focus on the Family with one employee and a once-a-week radio broadcast aired on only 36 stations.

Now an international organization, the ministry is dedicated to preserving Judeo-Christian values and strengthening and encouraging families through the life-changing message of Jesus Christ. Focus ministries reach families worldwide through 10 separate radio broadcasts, two television news features, 13 publications, 18 Web sites, and a steady series of books and award-winning films and videos for people of all ages and interests.

We'd love to hear from you!

For more information about the ministry, or if we can be of help to your family, simply write to Focus on the Family, Colorado Springs, CO 80995 or call 1-800-A-FAMILY (1-800-232-6459). Friends in Canada may write Focus on the Family, P.O. Box 9800, Stn. Terminal, Vancouver, B.C. V6B 4G3 or call 1-800-661-9800. Visit our Web site—www.family.org—to learn more about Focus on the Family or to find out if there is an associate office in your country.

Strengthen and enrich your marriage with these Focus on the Family® relationship builders.

The Marriage Masterpiece

Now that you've discovered the richness to be had in "The Focus on the Family Marriage Series" Bible studies, be sure to read the book the series is based on. *The Marriage Masterpiece* takes a fresh appraisal of the exquisite design God has for a man and woman. Explaining the reasons why this union is meant to last a lifetime, it also shows how God's relationship with humanity is the model for marriage. Rediscover the beauty and worth of marriage in a new light with this thoughtful, creative book. A helpful study guide is included for group discussion. Hardcover.

The Love List

Marriage experts Drs. Les and Leslie Parrot present eight healthy habits that refresh, transform and restore the intimacy of your marriage relationship. Filled with practical suggestions, this book will help you make daily, weekly, monthly and yearly improvements in your marriage. Hardcover.

Capture His Heart/Capture Her Heart

Lysa TerKeurst has written two practical guides—one for wives and one for husbands—that will open your eyes to the needs, desires and longings of your spouse. These two books each offer eight essential criteria plus creative tips for winning and holding his or her heart. Paperback set.

• • •

Look for these special books in your Christian bookstore or request a copy by calling 1-800-A-FAMILY (1-800-232-6459). Friends in Canada may write Focus on the Family, P.O. Box 9800, Stn. Terminal, Vancouver, B.C. V6B 4G3 or call 1-800-661-9800.

Visit our Web site (www.family.org) to learn more about the ministry or find out if there is a Focus on the Family office in your country.